FOOL FOR LOVE

AND

THE SAD LAMENT OF PECOS BILL ON THE EVE OF KILLING HIS WIFE

other plays by Sam Shepard

Action
Angel City
Back Bog Beast Bait
Buried Child
Chicago
Cowboy Mouth
Cowboys #2
Curse of the Starving Class
Forensic and the Navigator
Fourteen Hundred Thousand
Geography of the Horsedreamer
The Holy Ghostly
Icarus's Mother
Killer's Head
La Turista
The Mad Dog Blues
Melodrama Play
Operation Sidewinder
Red Cross
The Rock Garden
Seduced
Suicide in B$^\flat$
The Tooth of Crime
True West
The Unseen Hand

FOOL FOR LOVE

BY

SAM SHEPARD

AND

THE SAD LAMENT OF
PECOS BILL ON THE EVE
OF KILLING HIS WIFE

Words by Sam Shepard
Music by
Sam Shepard & Catherine Stone

faber and faber

LONDON · BOSTON

First published in the USA in 1983
by City Lights Books, San Francisco
First published in Great Britain in 1984
by Faber and Faber Limited
3 Queen Square London WC1N 3AU

Printed in Great Britain by
Whitstable Litho Limited
Whitstable, Kent
All rights reserved

British Library Cataloguing in Publication Data

Shepard, Sam
Fool for love; and, The sad lament of Pecos Bill
on the eve of killing his wife
I. Title   II. Shepard, Sam. Sad lament of
Pecos Bill on the eve of killing his wife
812'.54   PS3569.H394
ISBN 0-571-13365-7

FOOL FOR LOVE

For Billy Pearson

"The proper response to love is to accept it. There is nothing to *do*."

—Archbishop Anthony Bloom

FOOL FOR LOVE was first performed at the Magic
Theater in San Francisco on February 8, 1983. It
was directed by Sam Shepard.

The cast was as follows:

MAY: Kathy Baker
EDDIE: Ed Harris
MARTIN: Dennis Ludlow
THE OLD MAN: Will Marchetti

FOOL FOR LOVE

This play is to be performed relentlessly without a break

SCENE

SCENE: Stark, low-rent motel room on the edge of the Mojave Desert. Faded green plaster walls. Dark brown linoleum floor. No rugs. Cast iron four poster single bed, slightly off center favoring stage right, set horizontally to audience. Bed covered with faded blue chenille bedspread. Metal table with well-worn yellow formica top. Two matching metal chairs in the 50s "S" shape design with yellow plastic seats and backs, also well-worn. Table set extreme down left (from actor's p.o.v.). Chairs set upstage and down right of table. Nothing on the table. Faded yellow exterior door in the center of the stage left wall. When this door is opened, a small orange porch light shines into room. Yellow bathroom door up right of the stage right wall. This door slightly ajar to begin with, revealing part of an old style porcelain sink, white towels, a general clutter of female belongings and allowing a yellow light to bleed onto stage. Large picture window dead center of upstage wall, framed by dirty, long, dark green plastic curtains. Yellow-orange light from a street lamp shines thru window.

Extreme down left, next to the table and chairs is a small extended platform on the same level as the stage. The floor is black and it's framed by black curtains. The only object on the platform is an old maple rocking chair facing upstage right. A pillow with no slipcover rests on the seat. An old horse blanket with holes is laced to the back of the rocker. The color of the blanket should be subdued — grays and blacks.

Lights fade to black on set. In the dark, Merle Haggard's tune, "Wake Up" from his "The Way I Am" album is heard. Lights begin to rise slowly on stage in the tempo of the song. Volume swells slightly with the lights until they arrive at their mark. The platform remains in darkness with only a slight spill from the stage lights. Three actors are revealed.

CHARACTERS

THE OLD MAN *sits in the rocker facing up right so he's just slightly profile to the audience. A bottle of whiskey sits on the floor beside him. He picks up bottle and pours whiskey into a styrofoam cup and drinks. He has a scraggly red beard, wears an old stained "open-road" Stetson hat (the kind with the short brim), a sun-bleached, dark quilted jacket with the stuffing coming out at the elbows, black and white checkered slacks that are too short in the legs, beat up, dark Western boots, an old vest and a pale green shirt. He exists only in the minds of* MAY *and* EDDIE, *even though they might talk to him directly and acknowledge his physical presence.* THE OLD MAN *treats them as though they all existed in the same time and place.*

MAY *sits on edge of bed facing audience, feet on floor, legs apart, elbows on knees, hands hanging limp and crossed between her knees, head hanging forward, face staring at floor. She is absolutely still and maintains this attitude until she speaks. She wears a blue denim full skirt, baggy white t-shirt and bare feet with a silver ankle bracelet. She's in her early thirties.*

EDDIE *sits in the upstage chair by the table, facing* MAY. *He wears muddy, broken down cowboy*

*boots with silver gaffer's tape wrapped around
them at the toe and instep, well-worn, faded,
dirty jeans that smell like horse sweat. Brown
western shirt with snaps. A pair of spurs dangles
from his belt. When he walks, he limps slightly
and gives the impression he's rarely off a horse.
There's a peculiar broken-down quality about his
body in general, as though he's aged long before
his time. He's in his late thirties.*

*On the floor, between his feet, is a leather bucking
strap like bronc riders use. He wears a bucking
glove on his right hand and works resin into the
glove from a small white bag. He stares at MAY as
he does this and ignores THE OLD MAN. As the
song nears the end of its fade, he leans over,
sticks his gloved hand into the handle of the
bucking strap and twists it so that it makes a
weird stretching sound from the friction of the
resin and leather. The song ends, lights up full.
He pulls his hand out and removes gloves.*

EDDIE: *(seated, tossing glove on the table.)* *(short pause)* May, look. May? I'm not goin' anywhere. See? I'm right here. I'm not gone. Look *(She won't.)* I don't know why you won't just look at me. You know it's me. Who else do you think it is. *(Pause)* You want some water or somethin'? Huh? *(He gets up slowly, goes cautiously to her, strokes her head softly, she stays still.)* May? Come on. You can't just sit around here like this. How long you been sittin' here anyway? You want me to go outside and get you something? Some potato chips or something? *(She suddenly grabs his closest leg with both arms and holds tight burying her head between his knees.)* I'm not gonna' leave. Don't worry. I'm not gonna' leave. I'm stayin' right here. I already told ya' that. *(She squeezes tighter to his leg, he just stands there, strokes her head softly.)* May? Let go, okay? Honey? I'll put you back in bed. Okay? *(She grabs his other leg and holds on tight to both.)* Come on. I'll put you in bed and make you some hot tea or somethin'. You want some tea? *(She shakes her head violently, keeps holding on.)* With lemon? Some Ovaltine? May, you gotta' let go of me now, okay? *(Pause, then she pushes him away and returns to her original position.)* Now just lay back and try to relax. *(He starts to try to push her back gently on the bed as he pulls back the blankets. She erupts furiously, leaping off bed and lashing out at him with her fists. He backs off. She returns to bed and stares at him wild-eyed and angry, faces him squarely.)*

EDDIE: *(after pause)* You want me to go? *(She shakes her head.)*

MAY: No!

EDDIE: Well, what do you want then?

MAY: You smell.

EDDIE: I smell.

MAY: You do.

EDDIE: I been drivin' for days.

MAY: Your fingers smell.

EDDIE: Horses.

MAY: Pussy.

EDDIE: Come on, May.

MAY: They smell like metal.

EDDIE: I'm not gonna' start this shit.

MAY: Rich pussy. Very clean.

EDDIE: Yeah, sure.

MAY: You know it's true.

EDDIE: I came to see if you were all right.

MAY: I don't need you!

EDDIE: Okay. *(turns to go, collects his glove and bucking strap)* Fine.

MAY: Don't go!

EDDIE: I'm goin'.

> *(He exits stage left door, slamming it behind him; the door booms.)*

MAY: *(agonized scream)* Don't go!!!

(She grabs pillow, clutching it to her chest then throws herself face down on bed, moaning and moving from one end of bed to the other on her elbows and knees. EDDIE is heard returning to stage left door outside. She leaps off bed clutching pillow, stands upstage right of bed, facing stage left door. EDDIE enters stage left door, banging it behind him. He's left the glove and bucking strap off stage They stand there facing each other for a second. He makes a move toward her. MAY retreats to extreme upstage right corner of room clutching pillow to her chest. EDDIE stays against left wall, facing her.)

EDDIE: What am I gonna' do? Huh? What am I supposed to do?

MAY: You know.

EDDIE: What.

MAY: You're gonna' erase me.

EDDIE: What're you talkin' about?

MAY: You're either gonna' erase me or have me erased.

EDDIE: Why would I want that? Are you kidding?

MAY: Because I'm in the way.

EDDIE: Don't be stupid.

MAY: I'm smarter than you are and you know it. I can smell your thoughts before you even think 'em.

(EDDIE moves along wall to upstage left corner. MAY holds her ground in opposite corner.)

EDDIE: May, I'm tryin' to take care of you. All right?

MAY: No, you're not. You're just guilty. Gutless and guilty.

EDDIE: Great.

(He moves down left to table, sticking close to wall.) (Pause)

MAY: *(quietly, staying in corner)* I'm gonna' kill her ya' know.

EDDIE: Who?

MAY: Who.

EDDIE: Don't talk like that.

(MAY slowly begins to move down stage right as EDDIE simultaneously moves up left. Both of them press the walls as they move)

MAY: I am. I'm gonna' kill her and then I'm gonna' kill you. Systematically. With sharp knives. Two separate knives. One for her and one for you. *(She slams wall with her elbow. Wall resonates.)* So the blood doesn't mix. I'm gonna' torture her first though. Not you. I'm just gonna' let you have it. Probably in the midst of a kiss. Right when you think everything's been healed up. Right in the moment when you're sure you've got me buffaloed. That's when you'll die.

(She arrives extreme down right at the very limits of the set. EDDIE in the extreme up left corner. Pause)

EDDIE: You know how many miles I went outa' my way just to come here and see you? You got any idea?

MAY: Nobody asked you to come.

EDDIE: Two thousand, four hundred and eighty.

MAY: Yeah? Where were you, Katmandu or something?

EDDIE: Two thousand, four hundred and eighty miles.

MAY: So what!

(He drops his head, stares at floor. Pause. She stares at him. He begins to move slowly down left, sticking close to wall as he speaks.)

EDDIE: I missed you. I did. I missed you more than anything I ever missed in my whole life. I kept thinkin' about you the whole time I was driving. Kept seeing you. Sometimes just a part of you.

MAY: Which part?

EDDIE: Your neck.

MAY: My neck?

EDDIE: Yeah.

MAY: You missed my neck?

EDDIE: I missed all of you but your neck kept coming up for some reason. I kept crying about your neck.

MAY: Crying?

EDDIE: *(He stops by stage left door. She stays down right.)* Yeah. Weeping. Like a little baby. Uncontrollable. It would just start up and stop and then start up all over again. For miles. I couldn't stop it. Cars would pass me on the road. People would stare at me. My face was all twisted up. I couldn't stop my face.

MAY: Was this before or after your little fling with the Countess?

EDDIE: *(He bangs his head into wall. Wall booms.)* There wasn't any fling with any Countess!

MAY: You're a liar.

EDDIE: I took her out to dinner once, okay?

MAY: Ha!

(She moves upstage right wall.)

EDDIE: Twice.

MAY: You were bumping her on a regular basis! Don't gimme that shit.

EDDIE: You can believe whatever you want.

MAY: *(she stops by bathroom door, opposite Eddie)* I'll believe the truth! It's less confusing.

(Pause)

EDDIE: I'm takin' you back, May.

(She tosses pillow on bed and moves to upstage right corner.)

MAY: I'm not going back to that idiot trailer if that's what you think.

EDDIE: I'm movin' it. I got a piece of ground up in Wyoming.

MAY: Wyoming? Are you crazy? I'm not moving to Wyoming. What's up there? Marlboro Men?

EDDIE: You can't stay here.

MAY: Why not? I got a job. I'm a regular citizen here now.

EDDIE: You got a job?

MAY: *(she moves back down to head of bed)* Yeah. What'd you think, I was helpless?

EDDIE: No. I mean — it's been a long time since you had a job.

MAY: I'm a cook.

EDDIE: A cook? You can't even flip an egg, can you?

MAY: I'm not talkin' to you anymore!

(She turns away from him, runs into bathroom, slams door behind her. EDDIE goes after her, tries door but she's locked it.)

EDDIE: *(at bathroom door)* May, I got everything worked out. I been thinkin' about this for weeks. I'm gonna' move the trailer. Build a little pipe corral to keep the horses. Have a big vegetable garden. Some chickens maybe.

MAY'S VOICE: *(unseen, behind bathroom door)* I hate chickens! I hate horses! I hate all that shit! You know that. You got me confused with somebody else. You keep comin' up here with this lame country dream life with chickens and vegetables and I can't stand any of it. It makes me puke to even think about it.

EDDIE: (EDDIE *has crossed stage left during this, stops at table.)* You'll get used to it.

MAY: *(enters from bathroom)* You're unbelievable!

(She slams bathroom door, crosses upstage to window.)

EDDIE: I'm not lettin' go of you this time, May.

(He sits in chair upstage of table.)

MAY: You never had a hold of me to begin with. *(pause)* How many times have you done this to me?

EDDIE: What.

MAY: Suckered me into some dumb little fantasy and then dropped me like a hot rock. How many times has that happened?

EDDIE: It's no fantasy.

MAY: It's all a fantasy.

EDDIE: And I never dropped you either.

MAY: No, you just disappeared!

EDDIE: I'm here now aren't I?

MAY: Well, praise Jesus God!

EDDIE: I'm gonna take care of you, May. I am. I'm gonna' stick with you no matter what. I promise.

MAY: Get outa' here.

(Pause)

EDDIE: What'd you have to go and run off for anyway.

MAY: Run off? Me?

EDDIE: Yeah. Why couldn't you just stay put. You knew I was comin' back to get you.

MAY: *(crossing down to head of bed)* What do you think it's like sittin' in a tin trailer for weeks on end with the wind ripping through it? Waitin' around for the Butane to arrive. Hiking down to the laundromat in the rain. Do you think that's thrilling or somethin'?

EDDIE: *(still sitting)* I bought you all those magazines.

MAY: What magazines?

EDDIE: I bought you a whole stack of those fashion magazines before I left. I thought you liked those. Those French kind.

MAY: Yeah, I especially liked the one with the Countess on the cover. That was real cute.

(Pause)

EDDIE: All right.

(He stands)

MAY: All right, what.

(He turns to go out stage left door.)

MAY: Where are you going?

EDDIE: Just to get my stuff outa' the truck. I'll be right back.

MAY: What're you movin' in now or something?

EDDIE: Well, I thought I'd spend the night if that's okay.

MAY: Are you kidding?

EDDIE: *(opens door)* Then I'll just leave, I guess.

MAY: *(she stands)* Wait.

> *(He closes door. They stand there facing each other for a while. She crosses slowly to him. She stops. He takes a few steps toward her. Stops. They both move closer. Stop. Pause as they look at each other. They embrace. Long, tender kiss. They are very soft with each other. She pulls away from him slightly. Smiles. She looks him straight in the eyes, then suddenly knees him in the groin with tremendous force. EDDIE doubles over and drops like a rock. She stands over him. Pause.)*

MAY: You can take it, right. You're a stuntman.

> *(She exits into bathroom, stage right, slams the door behind her. The door is amplified with microphones and a bass drum hidden in the frame so that each time an actor slams it, the door booms loud and long. Same is true for the stage left door. EDDIE remains on the floor holding his stomach in pain. Stage lights drop to half their intensity as a spot rises softly on THE OLD MAN. He speaks directly to EDDIE.)*

THE OLD MAN: I thought you were supposed to be a fantasist, right? Isn't that basically the deal with you? You dream things up. Isn't that true?

EDDIE: *(stays on floor)* I don't know.

THE OLD MAN: You don't know. Well, if you don't know I don't know who the hell else does. I wanna' show

you somethin'. Somethin' real, okay? Somethin'
actual.

EDDIE: Sure.

THE OLD MAN: Take a look at that picture on the wall
over there. *(He points at wall stage right. There is
no picture but EDDIE stares at the wall.)* Ya' see
that? Take a good look at that. Ya' see it?

EDDIE: *(staring at wall)* Yeah.

THE OLD MAN: Ya' know who that is?

EDDIE: I'm not sure.

THE OLD MAN: Barbara Mandrell. That's who that is.
Barbara Mandrell. You heard a' her?

EDDIE: Sure.

THE OLD MAN: Well, would you believe me if I told ya' I
was married to her?

EDDIE: *(pause)* No.

THE OLD MAN: Well, see, now that's the difference
right there. That's realism. I am actually married to
Barbara Mandrell in my mind. Can you understand that?

EDDIE: Sure.

THE OLD MAN: Good. I'm glad we have an
understanding.

*(THE OLD MAN drinks from his cup. Spot slowly
fades to black as stage lights come back up full.
These light changes are cued to the opening and
closing of doors. MAY enters from bathroom,*

closes door quietly. She is carrying a sleek red dress, panty hose, a pair of black high heels, a black shoulder purse and a hair brush. She crosses to foot of bed and throws the clothes on it. Hangs the purse on a bed post, sits on foot of bed her back to EDDIE and starts brushing her hair. EDDIE remains on floor. She finishes brushing her hair, throws brush on bed, then starts taking off her clothes and changing into the clothes she brought on stage. As she speaks to EDDIE and changes into the new clothes, she gradually transforms from her former tough drabness into a very sexy woman. This occurs almost unnoticeably in the course of her speech.)

MAY: *(very cold, quick, almost monotone voice like she's writing him a letter)* I don't understand my feelings. I really don't. I don't understand how I could hate you so much after so much time. How, no matter how much I'd like to not hate you, I hate you even more. It grows. I can't even see you now. All I see is a picture of you. You and her. I don't even know if the picture's real anymore. I don't even care. It's a made-up picture. It invades my head. The two of you. And this picture stings even more than if I'd actually seen you with her. It cuts me. It cuts me so deep I'll never get over it. And I can't get rid of this picture either. It just comes. Uninvited. Kinda' like a little torture. And I blame you more for this little torture than I do for what you did.

EDDIE: *(standing slowly)* I'll go.

MAY: You better.

EDDIE: Why?

MAY: You just better.

EDDIE: I thought you wanted me to stay.

MAY: I got somebody coming to get me.

EDDIE: *(short pause, on his feet)* Here?

MAY: Yeah, here. Where else?

EDDIE: *(makes a move toward her upstage)* You been seeing somebody?

MAY: *(she moves quickly down left, crosses right)* When was the last time we were together, Eddie? Huh? Can you remember that far back?

EDDIE: Who've you been seeing?

(He moves violently toward her.)

MAY: Don't you touch me! Don't you even think about it.

EDDIE: How long have you been seeing him!

MAY: What difference does it make!

(Short pause. He stares at her, then turns suddenly and exits out the stage left door and slams it behind him. Door booms.)

MAY: Eddie! Where are you going? Eddie!

(Short pause. She looks after EDDIE, then turns fast, moves upstage to window. She parts the Venetian blinds, looks out window, turns back into room. She rushes to upstage side of bed, gets down on hands and knees, pulls a suitcase out from under bed, throws it on top of bed, opens it. She rushes into bathroom, disappears, leaving

*door open. She comes back on with various items
of clothing, throws stuff into suitcase, turns as if to
go back into bathroom. Stops. She hears EDDIE
off left. She quickly shuts suitcase, slides it under
bed again, rushes around to downstage side of
bed. Sits on bed. Stands again. Rushes back into
bathroom, returns with hairbrush, slams
bathroom door. Starts brushing her hair as
though that's what she's been doing all along.
She sits on bed brushing her hair. EDDIE enters
stage left, slams door behind him, door booms. He
stands there holding a ten gauge shotgun in one
hand and a bottle of tequila in the other. He
moves toward bed, tosses shotgun on bed beside
her.)*

MAY: *(she stands, moves upstage, stops brushing her
hair)* Oh, wonderful. What're you gonna' do with
that?

EDDIE: Clean it.

(He opens the bottle.)

EDDIE: You got any glasses?

MAY: In the bathroom.

EDDIE: What're they doin' in the bathroom?

*(EDDIE crosses toward bathroom door with
bottle.)*

MAY: I keep everything in the bathroom. It's safer.

EDDIE: You want some a' this?

MAY: I'm on the wagon.

EDDIE: Good. 'Bout time.

(He exits into bathroom. MAY moves back to bed, stares at shotgun.)

MAY: Eddie, this is a very friendly person who's coming over here. He's not malicious in any way. *(pause)* Eddie?

EDDIE'S VOICE: *(off right)* Where's the damn glasses?

MAY: In the medicine cabinet!

EDDIE'S VOICE: What the hell're they doin' in the medicine cabinet!

(Sound of medicine cabinet being opened and slammed shut off right)

MAY: There's no germs in the medicine cabinet!

EDDIE'S VOICE: Germs.

MAY: Eddie, did you hear me?

(EDDIE enters with a glass, pouring tequila into it slowly until it's full as he crosses to table down left.)

MAY: Did you hear what I said, Eddie?

EDDIE: About what?

MAY: About the man who's coming over here.

EDDIE: What man?

MAY: Oh, brother.

(EDDIE sets bottle of tequila on table then sits in upstage chair. Takes a long drink from glass. He ignores THE OLD MAN.)

EDDIE: First off, it can't be very serious.

MAY: Oh, really? And why is that?

EDDIE: Because you call him a "man."

MAY: What am I supposed to call him?

EDDIE: A "guy" or something. If you called him a "guy", I'd be worried about it but since you call him a "man" you give yourself away. You're in a dumb situation with this guy by calling him a "man". You put yourself below him.

MAY: What in the hell do you know about it.

EDDIE: This guy's gotta' be a twerp. He's gotta' be a punk chump in a two dollar suit or somethin'.

MAY: Anybody who doesn't half kill themselves falling off horses or jumping on steers is a twerp in your book.

EDDIE: That's right.

MAY: And what're you supposed to be, a "guy" or a "man"?

(EDDIE *lowers his glass slowly. Stares at her. Pause. He smiles then speaks low and deliberately.*)

EDDIE: I'll tell you what. We'll just wait for this "man" to come over here. The two of us. We'll just set right here and wait. Then I'll let you be the judge.

MAY: Why is everything a big contest with you? He's not competing with you. He doesn't even know you exist.

EDDIE: You can introduce me.

MAY: I'm not introducing you. I am definitely not introducing you. He'd be very embarrassed to find me here with somebody else. Besides, I've only just met him.

EDDIE: Embarrassed?

MAY: Yes! Embarrassed. He's a very gentle person.

EDDIE: Is that right. Well, I'm a very gentle person myself. My feelings get easily damaged.

MAY: What feelings.

(EDDIE *falls silent, takes a drink, then gets up slowly with glass, leaves bottle on table, crosses to bed, sits on bed, sets glass on floor, picks up shotgun and starts dismantling it.* MAY *watches him closely.*)

MAY: You can't keep messing me around like this. It's been going on too long. I can't take it anymore. I get sick everytime you come around. Then I get sick when you leave. You're like a disease to me. Besides, you got no right being jealous of me after all the bullshit I've been through with you.

(Pause. EDDIE *keeps his attention on shotgun as he talks to her.*)

EDDIE: We've got a pact.

MAY: Oh, God.

EDDIE: We made a pact.

MAY: There's nothing between us now!

EDDIE: Then what're you so excited about?

MAY: I'm not excited.

EDDIE: You're beside yourself.

MAY: You're driving me crazy. You're driving me totally crazy!

EDDIE: You know we're connected, May. We'll always be connected. That was decided a long time ago.

MAY: Nothing was decided! You made all that up.

EDDIE: You know what happened.

MAY: You promised me that was finished. You can't start that up all over again. You promised me.

EDDIE: A promise can't stop something like that. It happened.

MAY: Nothing happened! Nothing ever happened!

EDDIE: Innocent to the last drop.

MAY: *(pause, controlled)* Eddie — will you please leave? Now.

EDDIE: You're gonna' find out one way or the other.

MAY: I want you to leave.

EDDIE: You didn't want me to leave before.

MAY: I want you to leave now. And it's not because of this man. It's just —

EDDIE: What.

MAY: Stupid. You oughta' know that by now.

EDDIE: You think so, huh?

MAY: It'll be the same thing over and over again. We'll be together for a little while and then you'll be gone.

EDDIE: I'll be gone.

MAY: You will. You know it. You just want me now because I'm seeing somebody else. As soon as that's over, you'll be gone again.

EDDIE: I didn't come here because you were seein' somebody else! I don't give a damn who you're seeing! You'll never replace me and you know it!

MAY: Get outa' here!

(Long silence. EDDIE lifts his glass and toasts her, then slowly drinks it dry. He sets glass down softly on floor.)

EDDIE: *(smiles at her)* All right.

(He rises slowly, picks up the sections of his shotgun. He stands there looking down at the shotgun pieces for a second. MAY moves slightly toward him.)

MAY: Eddie —

(His head jerks up and stares at her. She stops cold.)

EDDIE: You're a traitor.

(He exits left with shotgun. Slams door. Door booms. MAY runs toward door.)

MAY: Eddie!!

(She throws herself against stage left door. Her arms reach out and hug the walls. She weeps

*and slowly begins to move along the stage left
wall upstage to the corner, embracing the wall as
she moves and weeps.* THE OLD MAN *begins to
tell his story as* MAY *moves slowly along the wall.
He tells it directly to her as though she's a child.*
MAY *remains involved with her emotion of loss
and keeps moving clear around the room, hug-
ging the walls during the course of the story until
she arrives in the extreme downstage right corner
of the room. She sinks to her knees.)*

(Slowly, in the course of MAY'S *mourning, the
spotlight softly rises on* THE OLD MAN *and the
stage lights decrease to half again.)*

THE OLD MAN: Ya' know, one thing I'll never forget. I'll
never forget this as long as I live — and I don't even
know why I remember it exactly. We were drivin'
through Southern Utah once, I think it was. Me,
you and your mother — in that old Plymouth we
had. You remember that Plymouth? Had a white
plastic hood ornament on it. Replica of the May-
flower I think it was. Some kind a' ship. Anyway,
we'd been drivin' all night and you were sound
asleep in the front. And all of a sudden you woke up
crying. Just bustin' a gut over somethin'. I don't
know what it was. Nightmare or somethin'. Woke
your Mom right up and she climbed over the seat
in back there with you to try to get you settled
down. But you wouldn't shut up for hell or high
water. Just kept wailing away. So I stopped the
Plymouth by the side of the road. Middle a'
nowhere. I can't even remember where it was
exactly. Pitch black. I picked you up outa' the back

seat there and carried you into this field. Thought the cold air might quiet you down a little bit. But you just kept on howling away. Then, all of a sudden, I saw somethin' move out there. Somethin' bigger than both of us put together. And it started to move toward us kinda' slow.

(MAY *begins to crawl slowly on her hands and knees from down right corner toward bed. When she reaches bed, she grabs pillow and embraces it, still on her knees. She rocks back and forth embracing pillow as* OLD MAN *continues.)*

And then it started to get joined up by some other things just like it. Same shape and everything. It was so black out there I could hardly make out my own hand. But these things started to kinda' move in on us from all directions in a big circle. And I stopped dead still and turned back to the car to see if your mother was all right. But I couldn't see the car anymore. So I called out to her. I called her name loud and clear. And she answered me back from outa' the darkness. She yelled back to me. And just then these things started to "moo". They all started "mooing" away.

(*He makes the sound of a cow.*)

And it turns out, there we were, standin' smack in the middle of a goddamn herd of cattle. Well, you never heard a baby pipe down so fast in your life. You never made a peep after that. The whole rest of the trip.

(MAY *stops rocking abruptly. Suddenly* MAY *hears* EDDIE *off left. Stage lights pop back up.*

Spot on THE OLD MAN *cuts to black. She leaps to her feet, completely dropping her grief, hesitates a second, then rushes to chair upstage of table and sits. She takes a drink straight from the bottle, slams bottle down on table, leans back in the chair and stares at the bottle as though she's been sitting like that the whole time since he left.* EDDIE *enters fast from stage left door carrying two steer ropes. He slams door. Door booms. He completely ignores* MAY. *She completely ignores him and keeps staring at the bottle. He crosses upstage of bed, throws one of the ropes on bed and starts building a loop in the other rope, feeding it with the left hand so that it makes a snake-like zipping sound as it passes through the honda. Now he begins to pay attention to* MAY *as he continues fooling with the rope. She remains staring at the bottle of tequila.)*

EDDIE: Decided to jump off the wagon, huh?

(He spins the rope above his head in a flat horn-loop, then ropes one of the bedposts, taking up the slack with a sharp snap of the right hand. He takes the loop off the bedpost, rebuilds it, swings and ropes another bedpost. He continues this right around the bed, roping every post and never missing. MAY *takes another drink and sets bottle down quietly.)*

MAY: *(still not looking at him)* What're you doing?

EDDIE: Little practice. Gotta' stay in practice these days. There's kids out there ropin' calves in six seconds dead. Can you believe that? Six and no change. Flyin' off the saddle on the right hand side like a bunch a' Spider Monkeys. I'm tellin' ya', they got it down to a science.

(He continues roping bedposts, making his way around the bed in a circle)

MAY: *(Flatly, staring at bottle)* I thought you were leaving. Didn't you say you were leaving?

EDDIE: *(as he ropes)* Well, yeah, I was gonna'. But then it suddenly occurred to me in the middle of the parking lot out there that there probably isn't any man comin' over here at all. There probably isn't any "guy" or any "man" or anybody comin' over here. You just made all that up.

MAY: Why would I do that?

EDDIE: Just to get even.

(She turns to him slowly in chair, takes a drink, stares at him, then sets bottle on table.)

MAY: I'll never get even with you.

(He laughs, crosses to table, takes a deep drink from bottle, cocks his head back, gargles, swallows, then does a back flip across stage and crashes into stage right wall.)

MAY: So, now we're gonna' get real mean and sloppy, is that it? Just like old times.

EDDIE: Well, I haven't dropped the reins in quite a while ya' know. I've been real good. I have. No hooch. No slammer. No women. No nothin'. I been a pretty boring kind of a guy actually. I figure I owe it to myself. Once a once.

(He returns to roping the bedposts. She just stares at him from the chair.)

MAY: Why are you doing this?

EDDIE: I already told ya'. I need the practice.

MAY: I don't mean that.

EDDIE: Well, say what ya' mean then, honey.

MAY: Why are you going through this whole thing again like you're trying to impress me or something. Like we just met. This is the same crap you laid on me in High School.

EDDIE: *(still roping)* Well, it's just a little testimony of my love, see baby. I mean if I stopped trying to impress you, that'd mean it was all over, wouldn't it?

MAY: It *is* all over.

EDDIE: You're trying to impress me, too, aren't you?

MAY: You know me inside and out. I got nothing new to show you.

EDDIE: You got this guy comin' over. This new guy. That's very impressive. I woulda' thought you'd be hung out to dry by now.

MAY: Oh, thanks a lot.

EDDIE: What is he, a "younger man" or something?

MAY: It's none of your damn business.

EDDIE: Have you balled him yet?

(She throws him a mean glare and just pins him with her eyes.)

EDDIE: Have you? I'm just curious. *(pause)* You don't have to tell me. I already know.

MAY: You're just like a little kid, you know that? A jealous, little snot-nosed kid.

(EDDIE laughs, spits, makes a 'snot-nosed-kid' face, keeps roping bedposts.)

EDDIE: I hope this guy comes over. I really hope he does. I wanna' see him walk through that door.

MAY: What're you gonna' do?

(He stops roping, turns to her. He smiles.)

EDDIE: I'm gonna nail his ass to the floor. Directly.

(He suddenly ropes chair downstage, right next to MAY. He takes up slack and drags chair violently back toward bed. Pause. They stare at each other. MAY suddenly stands, goes to bedpost, grabs her purse, slings it on her shoulder and heads for stage left door.)

MAY: I'm not sticking around for this.

(She exits stage left door leaving it open. EDDIE runs off stage after her.)

EDDIE: Where're you goin'?

MAY: *(off left)* Take your hands off a' me!

EDDIE: *(off left)* Wait a second, wait a second. Just a second, okay?

(MAY *screams.* EDDIE *carries her back on stage screaming and kicking. He sets her down, slams door shut. She walks away from him stage right, straightening her dress.)*

EDDIE: Tell ya' what. I'll back off. I'll be real nice. I will. I promise. I'll be just like a little ole pussy cat, okay? You can introduce me to him as your brother or something. Well — maybe not your brother.

MAY: Maybe not.

EDDIE: Your cousin. Okay? I'll be your cousin. I just wanna' meet him is all. Then I'll leave. Promise.

MAY: Why do you want to meet him? He's just a friend.

EDDIE: Just to see where you stand these days. You can tell a lot about a person by the company they keep.

MAY: Look. I'm going outside. I'm going to the pay phone across the street. I'm calling him up and I'm telling him to forget about the whole thing. Okay?

EDDIE: Good. I'll pack up your stuff while you're gone.

MAY: I'm not going with you Eddie!

(Suddenly *headlights arc across the stage from upstage right, through the window. They slash across the audience, then dissolve off left. These should be two intense beams of piercing white light and not 'realistic' headlights.)*

MAY: Oh, great.

(She *rushes upstage to window, looks out.* EDDIE *laughs, takes a drink.)*

EDDIE: Why don't ya' run on out there. Go ahead. Run on out. Throw yourself into his arms or somethin'. Blow kisses in the moonlight.

(EDDIE *laughs, moves to bed, pulls a pair of old spurs off his belt. Sits. Starts putting spurs on his boots. It's important these spurs look old and used, with small rowels — not cartoon "cowboy" spurs.* MAY *goes into bathroom leaving door open.*)

MAY: *(off right)* What're you doing?

EDDIE: Puttin' my hooks on. I wanna' look good for this "man". Give him the right impression. I'm yer cousin after all.

MAY: *(entering from bathroom)* If you hurt him, Eddie —

EDDIE: I'm not gonna' hurt him. I'm a nice guy. Very sensitive, too. Very civilized.

MAY: He's just a date, you know. Just an ordinary date.

EDDIE: Yeah? Well, I'm gonna turn him into a fig.

(He *starts laughing so hard at his own joke that he rolls off the bed and crashes to the floor. He goes into a fit of laughter, pounding his fists into the floor.* MAY *makes a move toward the door, then stops and turns to* EDDIE.)

MAY: Eddie! Do me a favor. Just this once, okay?

EDDIE: *(laughing hard)* Anything you want honey. Anything you want.

(He *goes on laughing hysterically.*)

MAY: *(turning away from him)* Shit.

> *(She goes to stage left door and throws it open. Pitch black outside with only the porch light glowing. She stands in the doorway, staring out. Pause as EDDIE slowly gains control of himself and stops laughing. He stares at MAY.)*

EDDIE: *(still on floor)* What're you doing? *(Pause. MAY keeps looking out)* May?

MAY: *(staring out open door)* It's not him.

EDDIE: It's not, huh?

MAY: No, it's not.

EDDIE: Well, who is it then?

MAY: Somebody else.

EDDIE: *(slowly getting up and sitting on bed)* Yeah. It's probably not ever gonna' be "him". What're you tryin' to make me jealous for? I know you've been livin' alone.

MAY: It's a big, huge, extra-long, black Mercedes Benz.

EDDIE: *(pause)* Well, this is a motel, isn't it? People are allowed to park in front of a motel if they're stayin' here.

MAY: People who stay here don't drive a big, huge, extra-long, black, Mercedes Benz.

EDDIE: You don't, but somebody else might.

MAY: *(still at door)* This is not a black Mercedes Benz type of motel.

EDDIE: Well, close the damn door then and get back inside.

MAY: Somebody's sitting out there in that car looking straight at me.

EDDIE: *(stands fast)* What're they doing?

MAY: It's not a "they". It's a "she".

(EDDIE drops to floor behind bed.)

EDDIE: Well what's she doing, then?

MAY: Just sitting there. Staring at me.

EDDIE: Get away from the door, May.

MAY: *(turning toward him slowly)* You don't know anybody with a black Mercedes Benz by any chance, do you?

EDDIE: Get away from the door!

(Suddenly the white headlight beams slash across the stage through the open door. EDDIE rushes to door, slams it shut and pushes MAY aside. Just as he slams the door the sound of a large caliber magnum pistol explodes off left, followed immediately by the sound of shattering glass then a car horn blares and continues on one relentless note.)

MAY: *(yelling over the sound of horn)* Who is that! Who in the hell is that out there!

EDDIE: How should I know.

(EDDIE flips the light switch off by stage left door. Stage lights go black. Bathroom light stays on.)

MAY: Eddie!

EDDIE: Just get down will ya'! Get down on the floor!

(EDDIE *grabs her and tries to pull her down on the floor beside the bed. MAY struggles in the dark with him. Car horn keeps blaring. Headlights start popping back and forth from high beam to low beam, slashing across stage through the window now.*)

MAY: Who is that? Did you bring her with you! You sonofabitch!

(*She starts lashing out at* EDDIE, *fighting with him as he tries to drag her down on the floor.*)

EDDIE: I didn't bring anybody with me! I don't know who she is! I don't know where she came from! Just get down on the floor will ya'!

MAY: She followed you here! Didn't she! You told her where you were going and she followed you.

EDDIE: I didn't tell anybody where I was going. I didn't know where I was going 'til I got here.

MAY: You are gonna' pay for this! I swear to God. You are gonna' pay.

(EDDIE *finally pulls her down and rolls over on top of her so she can't get up. She slowly gives up struggling as he keeps her pinned to the floor. Car horn suddenly stops. Headlights snap off. Long pause. They listen in the dark.*)

MAY: What do you think she's doing?

EDDIE: How should I know.

MAY: Don't pretend you don't know her. That's the kind of car a Countess drives. That's the kind of car I always pictured her in. *(She starts struggling again.)*

EDDIE: *(holding her down)* Just stay put.

MAY: I'm not gonna' lay here on my back with you on top of me and get shot by some dumb rich twat. Now lemme up, Eddie!

(Sound of tires burning rubber off left. Headlights arc back across the stage again from left to right. A car drives off. Sound fades.)

EDDIE: Just stay down!

MAY: I'm down!

(Long pause in the dark. They listen.)

MAY: How crazy is this chick anyway?

EDDIE: She's pretty crazy.

MAY: Have you balled her yet? *(pause)*

(EDDIE gets up slowly, hunched over crosses upstage to window cautiously, parts Venetian blinds and peeks outside.)

EDDIE: *(looking out)* Shit, she's blown the windshield outa' my truck. Goddamnit.

MAY: *(still on floor)* Eddie?

EDDIE: *(still looking out window)* What?

MAY: Is she gone?

EDDIE: I don't know. I can't see any headlights. *(pause)* I don't believe it.

MAY: *(gets up, crosses to light switch.)* Yeah, you shoulda' thought of the consequences before you got in her pants.

(She switches the lights back on. EDDIE whirls around toward her. He stands.)

EDDIE: *(moving toward her)* Turn the lights off! Keep the lights off!

(He rushes to light switch and turns lights back off. Stage goes back to darkness. MAY shoves past him and turns the lights back on again. Stage lit.)

MAY: This is my place!

EDDIE: Look, she's gonna' come back here. I know she's gonna' come back. We either have to get outa' here now or you have to keep the fuckin' lights off.

MAY: I thought you said you didn't know her!

EDDIE: Get your stuff! We're gettin' outa' here.

MAY: I'm not leaving! This is your mess, not mine.

EDDIE: I came here to get you! Whatsa' matter with you! I came all this way to get you! Do you think I'd do that if I didn't love you! Huh? That bitch doesn't mean anything to me! Nuthin'. I got no reason to be here but you.

MAY: I'm not goin', Eddie.

(Pause. EDDIE stares at her.)

(Spot rises on OLD MAN. *Stage lights stay the same.* EDDIE *and* MAY *just stand there staring at each other through the duration of* THE OLD MAN'S *words. They are not 'frozen', they just stand there and face each other in a suspended moment of recognition.)*

THE OLD MAN: Amazing thing is, neither one a' you look a bit familiar to me. Can't figure that one out. I don't recognize myself in either one a' you. Never did. 'Course your mothers both put their stamp on ya'. That's plain to see. But my whole side a' the issue is absent, in my opinion. Totally unrecognizable. You could be anybody's. Probably are. I can't even remember the original circumstances. Been so long. Probably a lot a' things I forgot. Good thing I got out when I did though. Best thing I ever did.

(Spot fades on OLD MAN. *Stage lights come back up.* EDDIE *picks up his rope and starts to coil it up.* MAY *watches him.)*

EDDIE: I'm not leavin'. I don't care what you think anymore. I don't care what you feel. None a' that matters. I'm not leavin'. I'm stayin' right here. I don't care if a hundred "dates" walk through that door — I'll take every one of 'em on. I don't care if you hate my guts. I don't care if you can't stand the sight of me or the sound of me or the smell of me. I'm never leavin'. You'll never get rid of me. You'll never escape me either. I'll track you down no matter where you go. I know exactly how your mind works. I've been right every time. Every single time.

MAY: You've gotta' give this up, Eddie.

EDDIE: I'm not giving it up!

(*Pause*)

MAY: (*calm*) Okay. Look. I don't understand what you've got in your head anymore. I really don't. I don't get it. *Now*, you desperately need me. *Now*, you can't live without me. *NOW*, you'll do anything for me. Why should I believe it this time?

EDDIE: Because it's true.

MAY: It was supposed to have been true every time before. Every other time. Now it's true again. You've been jerking me off like this for fifteen years. Fifteen years I've been a yo-yo for you. I've never been split. I've never been two ways about you. I've either loved you or not loved you. And now I just plain don't love you. Understand? Do you understand that? I don't love you. I don't need you. I don't want you. Do you get that? Now if you can still stay then you're either crazy or pathetic.

(*She crosses down left to table, sits in upstage chair facing audience, takes slug of tequila from bottle, slams it down on table. Headlights again come slashing across the stage from up right, across audience then disappear off left. EDDIE rushes to light switch, flips it off. Stage goes black. Exterior lights shine through.*)

EDDIE: (*taking her by shoulder*) Get in the bathroom!

MAY: (*pulls away*) I'm not going in the bathroom! I'm not gonna' hide in my own house! I'm gonna' go out there. I'm gonna' go out there and tear her damn head off! I'm gonna' wipe her out!

(She moves toward stage left door. EDDIE stops her. She screams. They struggle as MAY yells at stage left door.)

MAY: *(yelling at door)* Come on in here! Come on in here and bring your dumb gun! You hear me? Bring all your weapons and your skinny silly self! I'll eat you alive!

(Suddenly the stage left door bursts open and MARTIN crashes onstage in the darkness. He's in his mid-thirties, solidly built, wears a green plaid shirt, baggy work pants with suspenders, heavy work boots. MAY and EDDIE pull apart. MARTIN tackles EDDIE around the waist and the two of them go crashing into the stage right bathroom door. The door booms. MAY rushes to light switch, flips it on. Lights come back up on stage. MARTIN stands over EDDIE who's crumpled up against the wall on the floor. MARTIN is about to smash EDDIE in the face with his fist. MAY stops him with her voice.)

MAY: Martin, wait!

(Pause. MARTIN turns and looks at MAY. EDDIE is dazed, remains on floor. MAY goes to MARTIN and pulls him away from EDDIE.)

MAY: It's okay, Martin. It's uh — It's okay. We were just having a kind of an argument. Really. Just take it easy. All right?

(MARTIN moves back away from EDDIE. EDDIE stays on floor. Pause.)

MARTIN: Oh. I heard you screaming when I drove up and then all the lights went off. I thought some-body was trying to —

MAY: It's okay. This is my uh — cousin. Eddie.

MARTIN: *(stares at EDDIE)* Oh. I'm sorry.

EDDIE: *(grins at MARTIN)* She's lying.

MARTIN: *(looks at MAY)* Oh.

MAY: *(moving to table)* Everything's okay, Martin. You want a drink or something? Why don't you have a drink.

MARTIN: Yeah. Sure.

EDDIE: *(stays on floor)* She's lying through her teeth.

MAY: I gotta' get some glasses.

    (MAY exits quickly into bathroom, stepping over EDDIE. MARTIN stares at EDDIE. EDDIE grins back. Pause.)

EDDIE: She keeps the glasses in the bathroom. Isn't that weird?

    (MAY comes back on with two glasses. She goes to table, pours two drinks from bottle)

MAY: I was starting to think you weren't going to show up, Martin.

MARTIN: Yeah, I'm sorry. I had to water the football field down at the High School. Forgot all about it.

EDDIE: Forgot all about what?

MARTIN: I mean I forgot all about watering. I was half-way here when I remembered. Had to go back.

EDDIE: Oh, I thought you meant you forgot all about her.

MARTIN: Oh, no.

EDDIE: How far was halfway?

MARTIN: Excuse me?

EDDIE: How far were you when it was halfway here?

MARTIN: Oh — uh — I don't know. I guess a couple miles or so.

EDDIE: Couple miles? That's all? Couple a' lousy little miles? You wanna' know how many miles I came? Huh?

MAY: We've been drinking a little bit, Martin.

EDDIE: She hasn't touched a drop.

(Pause)

MAY: *(offering drink to* MARTIN*)* Here.

EDDIE: Yeah, that's my tequila, Martin.

MARTIN: Oh.

EDDIE: I don't care if you drink it. I just want you to know where it comes from.

MARTIN: Thanks.

EDDIE: You don't have to thank me. Thank the Mexicans. They made it.

MARTIN: Oh.

EDDIE: You should thank the entire Mexican nation in fact. We owe everything to Mexico down here. Do you realize that? You probably don't realize that do ya'. We're sittin' on Mexican ground right now. It's only by chance that you and me aren't Mexican ourselves. What kinda' people do you hail from anyway, Martin?

MARTIN: Me? Uh — I don't know. I was adopted.

EDDIE: Oh. You must have a lota' problems then, huh?

MARTIN: Well — not really, no.

EDDIE: No? You orphans are supposed to steal a lot aren't ya'? Shoplifting and stuff. You're also supposed to be the main group responsible for bumping off our Presidents.

MARTIN: Really? I never heard that.

EDDIE: Well, you oughta' read the papers, Martin.

(Pause)

MARTIN: I'm really sorry I knocked you over. I mean, I thought she was in trouble or something.

EDDIE: She is in trouble.

MARTIN: *(looks at MAY)* Oh.

EDDIE: She's in big trouble.

MARTIN: What's the matter, May?

MAY: *(moves to bed with drink, sits)* Nothing.

MARTIN: How come you had the lights off?

MAY: We were uh — just about to go out.

MARTIN: You were?

MAY: Yeah — well, I mean, we were going to come back.

(MARTIN *stands there between them. He looks at*
EDDIE, *then back to* MAY. *Pause.*)

EDDIE: *(laughs)* No, no, no. That's not what we were
gonna' do. Your name's Martin, right?

MARTIN: Yeah, right.

EDDIE: That's not what we were gonna' do, Marty.

MARTIN: Oh.

EDDIE: Could you hand me that bottle, please?

MARTIN: *(crossing to bottle at table)* Sure.

EDDIE: Thanks.

(MARTIN *moves back to* EDDIE *with bottle and
hands it to him.* EDDIE *drinks.*)

EDDIE: *(after drink)* We were actually having an argument about you. That's what we were doin'.

MARTIN: About me?

EDDIE: Yeah. We were actually in the middle of a big
huge argument about you. It got so heated up we
had to turn the lights off.

MARTIN: What was it about?

EDDIE: It was about whether or not you're actually a
man or not. Ya' know? Whether you're a "man" or
just a "guy".

(*Pause.* MARTIN *looks at* MAY. MAY *smiles
politely.* MARTIN *looks back to* EDDIE.)

EDDIE: See, she says you're a man. That's what she
calls you. A "man". Did you know that? That's what
she calls you.

MARTIN: *(looks back to* MAY*)* No.

MAY: I never called you a man, Martin. Don't worry
about it.

MARTIN: It's okay. I don't mind or anything.

EDDIE: No, but see I uh — told her she was fulla' shit. I
mean I told her that way before I even saw you. And
now that I see you I can't exactly take it back. Ya'
see what I mean, Martin?

(Pause, MAY *stands.)*

MAY: Martin, do you want to go to the movies?

MARTIN: Well, yeah — I mean, that's what I thought we
were going to do.

MAY: So let's go to the movies.

(She crosses fast to bathroom, steps over EDDIE,
*goes into bathroom, slams door, door booms.
Pause as* MARTIN *stares at bathroom door.*
EDDIE *stays on floor, grins at* MARTIN.*)*

MARTIN: She's not mad or anything is she?

EDDIE: You got me, buddy.

MARTIN: I didn't mean to make her mad.

(Pause)

EDDIE: What're you gonna' go see, Martin?

MARTIN: I can't decide.

EDDIE: What d'ya' mean you can't decide? You're supposed to have all that worked out ahead of time
aren't ya?

MARTIN: Yeah, but I'm not sure what she likes.

EDDIE: What's that got to do with it? You're takin' her
out to the movies, right?

MARTIN: Yeah.

EDDIE: So you pick the movie, right? The guy picks the
movie. The guy's always supposed to pick the
movie.

MARTIN: Yeah, but I don't want to take her to see something she doesn't want to see.

EDDIE: How do you know what she wants to see?

MARTIN: I don't. That's the reason I can't decide. I
mean what if I take her to something she's already
seen before?

EDDIE: You miss the whole point, Martin. The reason
you're taking her out to the movies isn't to see
something she hasn't seen before.

MARTIN: Oh.

EDDIE: The reason you're taking her out to the movies
is because you just want to be with her. Right? You
just wanna' be close to her. I mean you could take
her just about anywhere.

MARTIN: I guess.

EDDIE: I mean after a while you probably wouldn't
have to take her out at all. You could just hang
around here.

MARTIN: What would we do here?

EDDIE: Well, you could uh — tell each other stories.

MARTIN: Stories?

EDDIE: Yeah.

MARTIN: I don't know any stories.

EDDIE: Make 'em up.

MARTIN: That'd be lying wouldn't it?

EDDIE: No, no. Lying's when you believe it's true. If you already know it's a lie, then it's not lying.

MARTIN: *(after pause)* Do you want some help getting up off the floor?

EDDIE: I like it down here. Less tension. You notice how when you're standing up, there's a lot more tension?

MARTIN: Yeah. I've noticed that. A lot of times when I'm working, you know, I'm down on my hands and knees.

EDDIE: What line a' work do you follow, Martin?

MARTIN: Yard work mostly. Maintenance.

EDDIE: Oh, lawns and stuff?

MARTIN: Yeah.

EDDIE: You do lawns on your hands and knees?

MARTIN: Well — edging. You know, trimming around the edges.

EDDIE: Oh.

MARTIN: And weeding around the sprinkler heads. Stuff like that.

EDDIE: I get ya'.

MARTIN: But I've always noticed how much more relaxed I get when I'm down low to the ground like that.

EDDIE: Yeah. Well, you could get down on your hands and knees right now if you want to. I don't mind.

MARTIN: *(grins, gets embarrassed, looks at bathroom door)* Naw, I'll stand. Thanks.

EDDIE: Suit yourself. You're just gonna' get more and more tense.

(Pause)

MARTIN: You're uh — May's cousin, huh?

EDDIE: See now, right there. Askin' me that. Right there. That's a result of tension. See what I mean?

MARTIN: What?

EDDIE: Askin' me if I'm her cousin. That's because you're tense you're askin' me that. You already know I'm not her cousin.

MARTIN: Well, how would I know that?

EDDIE: Do I look like her cousin.

MARTIN: Well, she said that you were.

EDDIE: *(grins)* She's lying.

(Pause)

MARTIN: Well — what are you then?

EDDIE: *(laughs)* Now you're really gettin' tense, huh?

MARTIN: Look, maybe I should just go or something. I mean —

(MARTIN *makes a move to exit stage left. EDDIE rushes to stage left door and beats MARTIN to it. MARTIN freezes then runs to window upstage, opens it and tries to escape. EDDIE runs to him and catches him by the back of the pants, pulls him out of the window, slams him up against stage right wall then pulls him slowly down the wall as he speaks. They arrive at down right corner.)*

EDDIE: No, no. Don't go, Martin. Don't go. You'll just get all blue and lonely out there in the black night. I know. I've wandered around lonely like that myself. Awful. Just eats away at ya'. *(He puts his arm around MARTIN'S shoulder and leads him to table down left.)* Now just come on over here and sit down and we'll have us a little drink. Okay?

MARTIN: *(as he goes with EDDIE)* Uh — do you think she's okay in there?

EDDIE: Sure she's okay. She's always okay. She just likes to take her time. Just to torture you.

MARTIN: Well — we were supposed to go to the movies.

EDDIE: She'll be out. Don't worry about it. She likes the movies.

(They sit at table, down left. EDDIE pulls out the down right chair and seats MARTIN in it, then he goes to the upstage chair and sits so that he's now partially facing THE OLD MAN. Spot rises softly

on THE OLD MAN *but* MARTIN *does not acknowledge his presence. Stage lights stay the same. MARTIN sets his glass on table. EDDIE fills it up with the bottle.* THE OLD MAN'S *left arm slowly descends and reaches across the table holding out his empty styrofoam cup for a drink. EDDIE looks* THE OLD MAN *in the eye for a second then pours him a drink, too. All three of them drink. EDDIE takes his from the bottle.)*

MARTIN: What exactly's the matter with her anyway?

EDDIE: She's in a state a' shock.

(THE OLD MAN chuckles to himself. Drinks.)

MARTIN: Shock? How come?

EDDIE: Well, we haven't seen each other in a long time. I mean — me and her, we go back quite a ways, see. High School.

MARTIN: Oh. I didn't know that.

EDDIE: Yeah. Lota' miles.

MARTIN: And you're not really cousins?

EDDIE: No. Not really. No.

MARTIN: You're — her husband?

EDDIE: No. She's my sister. *(He and* THE OLD MAN *look at each other then he turns back to* MARTIN.) My half-sister.

(Pause. EDDIE and OLD MAN drink.)

MARTIN: Your sister?

EDDIE: Yeah.

MARTIN: Oh. So — you knew each other even before High School then, huh?

EDDIE: No, see, I never even knew I had a sister until it was too late.

MARTIN: How do you mean?

EDDIE: Well, by the time I found out we'd already — you know — fooled around.

(OLD MAN *shakes his head, drinks. Long pause.* MARTIN *just stares at* EDDIE.)

EDDIE: *(grins)* Whatsa' matter, Martin?

MARTIN: You fooled around?

EDDIE: Yeah.

MARTIN: Well — um — that's illegal, isn't it?

EDDIE: I suppose so.

THE OLD MAN: *(to* EDDIE) Who is this guy?

MARTIN: I mean — is that true? She's really your sister?

EDDIE: Half. Only half.

MARTIN: Which half?

EDDIE: Top half. In horses we call that the "topside".

THE OLD MAN: Yeah, and the mare's what? The mare's uh — "distaff", isn't it? Isn't that the bottom half? "Distaff." Funny I should remember that.

MARTIN: And you fooled around in High School together?

EDDIE: Yeah. Sure. Everybody fooled around in High School. Didn't you?

MARTIN: No. I never did.

EDDIE: Maybe you should have, Martin.

MARTIN: Well, not with my sister.

EDDIE: No, I wouldn't recommend that.

MARTIN: How could that happen? I mean —

EDDIE: Well, see— *(pause, he stares at* OLD MAN*)* — our Daddy fell in love twice. That's basically how it happened. Once with my mother and once with her mother.

THE OLD MAN: It was the same love. Just got split in two, that's all.

MARTIN: Well, how come you didn't know each other until High School, then?

EDDIE: He had two separate lives. That's how come. Two completely separate lives. He'd live with me and my mother for a while and then he'd disappear and go live with her and her mother for a while.

THE OLD MAN: Now don't be too hard on me, boy. It can happen to the best of us.

MARTIN: And you never knew what was going on?

EDDIE: Nope. Neither did my mother.

THE OLD MAN: She knew.

EDDIE: *(to* MARTIN*)* She never knew.

MARTIN: She must've suspected something was going on.

EDDIE: Well, if she did she never let on to me. Maybe she was afraid of finding out. Or maybe she just loved him. I don't know. He'd disappear for months at a time and she never once asked him where he went. She was always glad to see him when he came back. The two of us used to go running out of the house to meet him as soon as we saw the Studebaker coming across the field.

THE OLD MAN: *(to* EDDIE*)* That was no Studebaker, that was a Plymouth. I never owned a goddamn Studebaker.

EDDIE: This went on for years. He kept disappearing and reappearing. For years that went on. Then, suddenly, one day it stopped. He stayed home for a while. Just stayed in the house. Never went outside. Just sat in his chair. Staring. Then he started going on these long walks. He'd walk all day. Then he'd walk all night. He'd walk out across the fields. In the dark. I used to watch him from my bedroom window. He'd disappear in the dark with his overcoat on.

MARTIN: Where was he going?

EDDIE: Just walking.

THE OLD MAN: I was making a decision.

(EDDIE gets MARTIN to his feet and takes him on a walk around the entire stage as he tells the story. MARTIN *is reluctant but* EDDIE *keeps pulling him along.)*

EDDIE: But one night I asked him if I could go with him. And he took me. We walked straight out across the fields together. In the dark. And I remember it was just plowed and our feet sank down in the powder and the dirt came up over the tops of my shoes and weighed me down. I wanted to stop and empty my shoes out but he wouldn't stop. He kept walking straight ahead and I was afraid of losing him in the dark so I just kept up as best I could. And we were completely silent the whole time. Never said a word to each other. We could barely see a foot in front of us, it was so dark. And these white owls kept swooping down out of nowhere, hunting for jackrabbits. Diving right past our heads, then disappearing. And we just kept walking silent like that for miles until we got to town. I could see the drive-in movie way off in the distance. That was the first thing I saw. Just square patches of color shifting. Then vague faces began to appear. And, as we got closer, I could recognize one of the faces. It was Spencer Tracy. Spencer Tracy moving his mouth. Speaking without words. Speaking to a woman in a red dress. Then we stopped at a liquor store and he made me wait outside in the parking lot while he bought a bottle. And there were all these Mexican migrant workers standing around a pick-up truck with red mud all over the tires. They were drinking beer and laughing and I remember being jealous of them and I didn't know why. And I remember seeing the old man through the glass door of the liquor store as he paid for the bottle. And I remember feeling sorry for him and I didn't know why. Then he came outside with the bottle wrapped in a brown paper sack and as soon as he came out, all the Mexican men stopped laughing. They just stared at us as we walked away.

(During the course of the story the lights shift down very slowly into blues and greens — moonlight.)

EDDIE: And we walked right through town. Past the donut shop, past the miniature golf course, past the Chevron station. And he opened the bottle up and offered it to me. Before he even took a drink, he offered it to me first. And I took it and drank it and handed it back to him. And we just kept passing it back and forth like that as we walked until we drank the whole thing dry. And we never said a word the whole time. Then, finally, we reached this little white house with a red awning, on the far side of town. I'll never forget the red awning because it flapped in the night breeze and the porch light made it glow. It was a hot, desert breeze and the air smelled like new cut alfalfa. We walked right up to the front porch and he rang the bell and I remember getting real nervous because I wasn't expecting to visit anybody. I thought we were just out for a walk. And then this woman comes to the door. This real pretty woman with red hair. And she throws herself into his arms. And he starts crying. He just breaks down right there in front of me. And she's kissing him all over the face and holding him real tight and he's just crying like a baby. And then through the doorway, behind them both, I see this girl. *(The bathrom door very slowly and silently swings open revealing MAY, standing in the door frame back-lit with yellow light in her red dress. She just watches* EDDIE *as he keeps telling story. He and Martin are unaware of her presence.)* She just appears. She's just standing there, staring at me and I'm staring back at her and we can't take our eyes off each other. It was like we knew each other from somewhere but we couldn't place where. But the second we saw each other, that very second, we knew we'd never stop being in love.

(MAY *slams bathroom door behind her. Door booms. Lights bang back up to their previous setting.)*

MAY: *(to EDDIE)* Boy, you really are incredible! You're unbelievable! Martin comes over here. He doesn't know you from Adam and you start telling him a story like that. Are you crazy? None of it's true, Martin. He's had this weird, sick idea for years now and it's totally made up. He's nuts. I don't know where he got it from. He's completely nuts.

EDDIE: *(to MARTIN)* She's kinda embarrassed about the whole deal, see. You can't blame her really.

MARTIN: I didn't even know you could hear us out here, May. I —

MAY: I heard every word. I followed it very carefully. He's told me that story a thousand times and it always changes.

EDDIE: I never repeat myself.

MAY: You do nothing but repeat yourself. That's all you do. You just go in a big circle.

MARTIN: *(standing)* Well, maybe I should leave.

EDDIE: NO! You sit down.

   (Silence. MARTIN slowly sits again)

EDDIE: *(quietly to MARTIN, leaning toward him)* Did you think that was a story, Martin? Did you think I made that whole thing up?

MARTIN: No. I mean, at the time you were telling it, it seemed real.

EDDIE: But now you're doubting it because she says it's a lie?

MARTIN: Well —

EDDIE: She suggests it's a lie to you and all of a sudden you change your mind? Is that it? You go from true to false like that, in a second?

MARTIN: I don't know.

MAY: Let's go to the movies, Martin.

   (MARTIN stands again)

EDDIE: Sit down!

   (MARTIN sits back down. Long pause)

MAY: Eddie —

   (Pause)

EDDIE: What?

MAY: We want to go to the movies. *(Pause. EDDIE just stares at her.)* I want to go out to the movies with Martin. Right now.

EDDIE: Nobody's going to the movies. There's not a movie in this town that can match the story I'm gonna tell. I'm gonna finish this story.

MAY: Eddie —

EDDIE: You wanna' hear the rest of the story, don't ya', Martin?

MARTIN: *(Pause. He looks at* MAY *then back to* EDDIE*)* Sure.

MAY: Martin, let's go. Please.

MARTIN: I —

(Long pause. EDDIE *and* MARTIN *stare at each other.)*

EDDIE: You what?

MARTIN: I don't mind hearing the rest of it if you want to tell the rest of it.

THE OLD MAN: *(to himself)* I'm dyin' to hear it myself.

*(*EDDIE *leans back in his chair. Grins.)*

MAY: *(to* EDDIE*)* What do you think this is going to do? Do you think this is going to change something?

EDDIE: No.

MAY: Then what's the point?

EDDIE: It's absolutely pointless.

MAY: Then why put everybody through this. Martin doesn't want to hear this bullshit. *I* don't want to hear it.

EDDIE: I know *you* don't wanna' hear it.

MAY: Don't try to pass it off on me! You got it all turned
      around, Eddie. You got it all turned around. You
      don't even know which end is up anymore. Okay.
      Okay. I don't need either of you. I don't need any of
      it because I already know the rest of the story. I
      know the whole rest of the story, see. *(She speaks
      directly to* EDDIE, *who remains sitting.)* I know it
      just exactly the way it happened. Without any little
      tricks added on to it.

      *(THE OLD MAN leans over to EDDIE,
      confidentially.)*

THE OLD MAN: What does she know?

EDDIE: *(to* OLD MAN) She's lying.

      *(Lights begin to shift down again in the course of
      MAY'S story. She moves very slowly downstage
      then crosses toward OLD MAN as she tells it.)*

MAY: You want me to finish the story for you, Eddie?
      Huh? You want me to finish this story? *(Pause as
      MARTIN sits again)* See, my mother — the pretty
      red-haired woman in the little white house with
      the red awning, was desperately in love with the old
      man. Wasn't she, Eddie? You could tell that right
      away. You could see it in her eyes. She was
      obsessed with him to the point where she couldn't
      stand being without him for even a second. She
      kept hunting for him from town to town. Following
      little clues that he left behind, like a postcard
      maybe, or a motel on the back of a matchbook. *(To
      MARTIN)* He never left her a phone number or an
      address or anything as simple as that because my
      mother was his secret, see. She hounded him for

years and he kept trying to keep her at a distance because the closer these two separate lives drew together, these two separate women, these two separate kids, the more nervous he got. The more filled with terror that the two lives would find out about each other and devour him whole. That his secret would take him by the throat. But finally she caught up with him. Just by a process of elimination she dogged him down. I remember the day we discovered the town. She was on fire. "This is it!" she kept saying; "this is the place!" Her whole body was trembling as we walked through the streets, looking for the house where he lived. She kept squeezing my hand to the point where I thought she'd crush the bones in my fingers. She was terrified she'd come across him by accident on the street because she knew she was trespassing. She knew she was crossing this forbidden zone but she couldn't help herself. We walked all day through that stupid hick town. All day long. We went through every neighborhood, peering through every open window, looking in at every dumb family, until finally we found him.

(Rest)

It was just exactly supper time and they were all sitting down at the table and they were having fried chicken. That's how close we were to the window. We could see what they were eating. We could hear their voices but we couldn't make out what they were saying. Eddie and his mother were talking but the old man never said a word. Did he, Eddie? Just sat there eating his chicken in silence.

THE OLD MAN: *(to* EDDIE) Boy, is she ever off the wall with this one. You gotta' do somethin' about this.

MAY: The funny thing was, that almost as soon as we'd found him — he disappeared. She was only with him about two weeks before he just vanished. Nobody saw him after that. Ever. And my mother — just turned herself inside out. I never could understand that. I kept watching her grieve, as though somebody'd died. She'd pull herself up into a ball and just stare at the floor. And I couldn't understand that because I was feeling the exact opposite feeling. I was in love, see. I'd come home after school, after being with Eddie, and I was filled with this joy and there she'd be — standing in the middle of the kitchen staring at the sink. Her eyes looked like a funeral. And I didn't know what to say. I didn't even feel sorry for her. All I could think of was him.

THE OLD MAN: *(to* EDDIE) She's gettin' way outa' line, here.

MAY: And all he could think of was me. Isn't that right, Eddie. We couldn't take a breath without thinking of each other. We couldn't eat if we weren't together. We couldn't sleep. We got sick at night when we were apart. Violently sick. And my mother even took me to see a doctor. And Eddie's mother took him to see the same doctor but the doctor had no idea what was wrong with us. He thought it was the flu or something. And Eddie's mother had no idea what was wrong with him. But my mother — my mother knew exactly what was wrong. She knew it clear down to her bones. She recognized every symptom. And she begged me not to see him but I wouldn't listen. Then she begged Eddie not to see me but he wouldn't listen. Then she went to Eddie's mother and begged her. And Eddie's mother — *(Pause. She looks straight at* EDDIE*)* — Eddie's mother blew her brains out. Didn't she, Eddie? Blew her brains right out.

THE OLD MAN: *(Standing. He moves from the platform onto the stage, between* EDDIE *and* MAY.*)* Now, wait a second! Wait a second. Just a goddamn second here. This story doesn't hold water. *(To* EDDIE *who stays seated.)* You're not gonna' let her off the hook with that one are ya'? That's the dumbest version I ever heard in my whole life. She never blew her brains out. Nobody ever told me that. Where the hell did that come from? *(To* EDDIE *who remains seated)* Stand up! Get on yer feet now goddamn it! I wanna' hear the male side a' this thing. You gotta' represent me now. Speak on my behalf. There's no one to speak for me now! Stand up!

(EDDIE stands slowly. Stares at OLD MAN*)*

Now tell her. Tell her the way it happened. We've got a pact. Don't forget that.

EDDIE: *(calmly to* OLD MAN*)* It was your shotgun. Same one we used to duck hunt with. Browning. She never fired a gun before in her life. That was her first time.

THE OLD MAN: Nobody told me any a' that. I was left completely in the dark.

EDDIE: You were gone.

THE OLD MAN: Somebody could've found me! Somebody could've hunted me down. I wasn't that impossible to find.

EDDIE: You were gone.

THE OLD MAN: That's right, I was gone! I was gone. You're right. But I wasn't disconnected. There was nothing cut off in me. Everything went on just the same as though I'd never left. *(to* MAY*)* But *your* mother —your mother wouldn't give it up, would she?

(THE OLD MAN moves toward MAY and speaks directly to her. MAY keeps her eyes on EDDIE who very slowly turns toward her in the course of THE OLD MAN'S speech. Once their eyes meet they never leave each other's gaze.)

THE OLD MAN: *(to* MAY*)* She drew me to her. She went out of her way to draw me in. She was a force. I told her I'd never come across for her. I told her that right from the very start. But she opened up to me. She wouldn't listen. She kept opening up her heart to me. How could I turn her down when she loved me like that? How could I turn away from her? We were completely whole.

(EDDIE and MAY just stand there staring at each other. THE OLD MAN moves back to EDDIE. Speaks to him directly.)

THE OLD MAN: *(to* EDDIE*)* What're you doin'? Speak to her. Bring her around to our side. You gotta' make her see this thing in a clear light.

(Very slowly EDDIE and MAY move toward each other.)

THE OLD MAN: *(to EDDIE)* Stay away from her! What the hell are you doin'! Keep away from her! You two can't come together! You gotta hold up my end a' this deal. I got nobody now! Nobody! You can't betray me! You gotta' represent me now! You're my son!

(EDDIE and MAY come together center stage. They embrace. They kiss each other tenderly. Headlights suddenly arc across stage again from upright, cutting across the stage through window then disappearing off left. Sound of loud collision, shattering glass, an explosion. Bright orange and blue light of a gasoline fire suddenly illuminates upstage window. Then sounds of horses screaming wildly, hooves galloping on pavement, fading, then total silence. Light of gas fire continues now to end of play. EDDIE and MAY never stop holding each other through all this. Long pause. No one moves. Then MARTIN stands and moves upstage to window, peers out through Venetian blinds. Pause.)

MARTIN: *(upstage at window, looking out into flames)* Is that your truck with the horse trailer out there?

EDDIE: *(stays with MAY)* Yeah.

MARTIN: It's on fire.

EDDIE: Yeah.

MARTIN: All the horses are loose.

EDDIE: *(steps back away from MAY)* Yeah, I figured.

MAY: Eddie —

EDDIE: *(to* MAY*)* I'm just gonna' go out and take a look. I gotta' at least take a look, don't I?

MAY: What difference does it make?

EDDIE: Well, I can't just let her get away with that. What am I supposed to do? *(moves toward stage left door)* I'll just be a second.

MAY: Eddie —

EDDIE: I'm only gonna' be a second. I'll just take a look at it and I'll come right back. Okay?

(EDDIE exits stage left door. MAY stares at door, stays where she is. MARTIN stays upstage. MARTIN turns slowly from window upstage and looks at MAY. Pause. MAY moves to bed, pulls suitcase out from underneath, throws it on bed and opens it. She goes into bathroom and comes out with clothes. She packs the clothes in suitcase. MARTIN watches her for a while then moves slowly downstage to her as she continues.)

MARTIN: May —

(MAY goes back into bathroom and comes back out with more clothes. She packs them.)

MARTIN: Do you need some help or anything? I got a car. I could drive you somewhere if you want. *(Pause.* MAY *just keeps packing her clothes.)* Are you going to go with him?

(She stops. Straightens up. Stares at MARTIN. Pause.)

MAY: He's gone.

MARTIN: He said he'd be back in a second.

MAY: *(Pause)* He's gone.

> *(MAY exits with suitcase out stage left door. She leaves the door open behind her. MARTIN just stands there staring at open door for a while. THE OLD MAN looks stage left at his rocking chair then a little above it, in blank space. Pause. OLD MAN starts moving slowly back to platform.)*

THE OLD MAN: *(pointing into space, stage left)* Ya' see that picture over there? Ya' see that? Ya' know who that is? That's the woman of my dreams. That's who that is. And she's mine. She's all mine. Forever.

> *(He reaches rocking chair, sits, but keeps staring at imaginary picture. He begins to rock very slowly in the chair. After OLD MAN sits in rocker, Merle Haggard's "I'm the One who Loves You" starts playing as lights begin a very slow fade. MARTIN moves slowly upstage to window and stops. He stares out with his back to audience. The fire glows through window as stage lights fade. OLD MAN keeps rocking slowly. Stage lights keep fading slowly to black. Fire glows for a while in the dark then cuts to black. Song continues in dark and swells in volume.)*

END

THE SAD LAMENT OF PECOS BILL
ON THE EVE OF KILLING HIS WIFE

For O-Lan

*THE SAD LAMENT OF PECOS BILL ON THE EVE
OF KILLING HIS WIFE* was first performed at the
first Bay Area Playwrights' Festival at the Palace of
the Legion of Honor in San Franciso on October 22,
1976. It was directed by Robert Woodruff.

The cast was as follows:

BILL: Emil Borelli
SUE: Sigurd Wurschmidt

Words by Sam Shepard
Music by Sam Shepard and Catherine Stone

Arranged by the Overtone Theater

Orchestrated for guitar, bass, drums, piano,
pedal steel, saw, harmonica, harp, synthesizer,
fiddle

THE SAD LAMENT OF PECOS BILL
ON THE EVE OF KILLING HIS WIFE

(SCENE: Bare, Open Stage. As much room as possible in all directions. A scrim covering entire upstage wall which can be back-lit. The stage starts out in total darkness. Music begins in the darkness, slowly building in intensity. As the music swells, an apricot sunset slowly emerges on the scrim. As the light from the sunset reaches its mid-point, PECOS BILL appears from the up-left corner pulling a giant catfish on a rope. His costume is a tall, ten gallon cowboy hat, a black leather vest with silver conchos, red cowboy shirt, green bandana around his neck, black and white pony skin chaps, cowboy boots and silver spurs, two six shooters on his waist, brown fringed gloves. PECOS is short. Lying on her back, on top of the catfish, is his wife, SLUE-FOOT SUE. Her costume is a white wedding gown, a rose in her hair and bare feet. She is dead but sings anyway. PECOS slowly drags the catfish toward center stage. All the words are sung.

Opening: THE STAMPEDE OF FATE

Driving ♩ = 160

Cm
Band vamps   BILL: Oh why, on such a   day as   this   my

Fm   Cm
darlin Slue Foot   Sue   did you force me   wild   and

Cm   Fm
foolish- ly   to be the cause of   buryin you   SUE: It

G♭   Gm
was my fate   you   saw me there   ridin high on the Rio Grande

Gm   C⁷
            a-   top some slimey   catfish back   you were

F   G   Cm
callin for my   hand   BILL: I was   blinded by   the

Cm   Fm   Cm
sight of you   No such a woman did   exist   I'd

Cm
never seen   the   like of it   ridin high on some big old fish

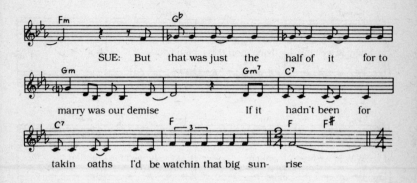

SUE: But that was just the half of it for to
marry was our demise If it hadn't been for
takin oaths I'd be watchin that big sun- rise

BUT WASN'T IT ME

BILL: But wasn't it me who taught the bronco how to buck

SUE: And wasn't it you who roped tornados by the neck

BILL: And wasn't it me who dug the mighty Rio Grande

SUE: All by hand

BOTH: All by hand Then

STAMPEDE II

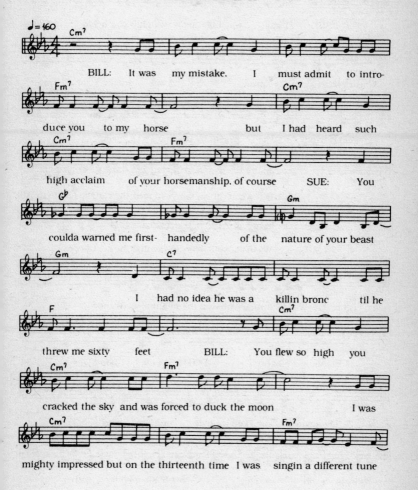

BILL: It was my mistake. I must admit to intro-

duce you to my horse but I had heard such

high acclaim of your horsemanship. of course SUE: You

coulda warned me first- handedly of the nature of your beast

I had no idea he was a killin bronc til he

threw me sixty feet BILL: You flew so high you

cracked the sky and was forced to duck the moon I was

mighty impressed but on the thirteenth time I was singin a different tune

SUE: I was way high above, watchin you below All the

earth was a tiny speck I was prayin for my

second wind I was prayin to save my neck

BILL: But wasn't it me who whipped the rattlesnake to death

SUE: Wasn't it you who in- vented the centipede

BILL: Wasn't it me who dug the mighty Rio Grande

SUE: All by hand BOTH: All by hand

Then why is we both dyin on this land

Why is we for- saken lost & shamed for- gotten

Why is we both rotten in the memories of man in the

memories of man in the memories of man

MILKY WAY

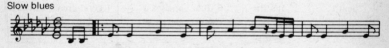

BILL: 1.   It was three whole days and four whole nights
                            and you were bouncin further

SUE: 2.   called him "Widow   Maker" but the re- verse was comin

BILL: 3.   fadin   fast in- side my chest my poor head was all on

SUE: 4.   that gun way down below and   I knew what you had in

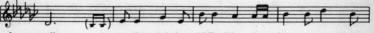

1.   still   out beyond the Milky Way but bronc ain't had his

2.   true   If I called him any- thing myself I'd a called the same to

3.   fire   I could not think but what to do so I pulled out that cold blue

4.   mind   To fire upon your dear sweet wife who was helplessly   re-

fill

you   2. You

iron   3. I was

signed 4. You drew

RECITATIVE

I FIRED AND FIRED

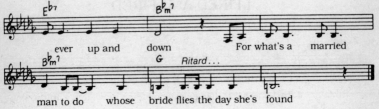

ever   up and   down   For what's a   married

man to do   whose   bride flies the day she's found

I AIN'T BLAMIN YOU

Slow and free

SUE: I ain't   blamin you my   darlin Bill   It   was in the hands of

time   to   have me die a mortal's death   to die in a hero's prime

IT'S ME AIN'T IT ME

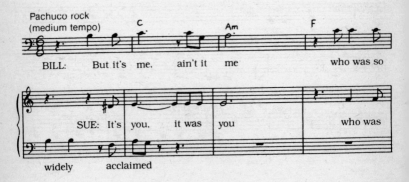

Pachuco rock
(medium tempo)

BILL: But it's   me,   ain't it   me   who was so

SUE: It's   you,   it was   you   who was

widely   acclaimed

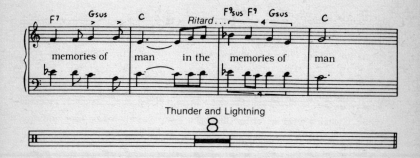

memories of man in the memories of man

Thunder and Lightning

NOW YOU'RE DEAD AND YOU'RE GONE

Recitative (slow, free)

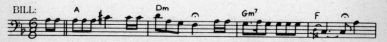

BILL:

Now you're dead and you're gone　　I can feel the cold sting of my guilt I
　　　　　　　and I'm just passin on

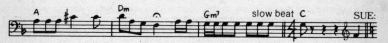

look for a place to bury you, sweet but I'm buried as sure as you're kilt　Don't

languish sweet Bill It's a　poisonous pill　What's done is all done and it's

through   Your crime was invented by   lies of   the   mind   It's a

crime   when a lie is so   true   BILL: But I was   fathered by liars   and my

offspring was too   Oh   how can I ever es-   cape it   To be

born as a legend and   die as a man   it's   painful to even

relate it— SUE: Be   kind on yourself   You   won't last forever and the

moon could care less what you do   But   don't forget *me* on the

day that you saw me   and how I was capturing   you

BUT AREN'T I A HERO

Recitative (quick and forceful)

BILL: But   aren't I a hero   above all that stuff How could I just fall by the

wayside   I'm   fixed in the prairies and valleys below me   I'm

fixed until heavens   collide   B⁹(♭13)

YOU'RE VANISHING BILLY

fff ......transforms into shimmer using this   chord voicing

Pedal point

SUE: You're vanish- ing   Billy   just

Pedal

look at your breath | Do you see it make | ripples in space

You're gone with the wind like others be-

fore you   Not even   leavin   a   trace

Not   even   leavin   a   trace

Fiddle

I'M BIGGER THAN TIME

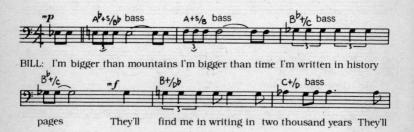

BILL: I'm bigger than mountains I'm bigger than time I'm written in history

pages   They'll   find me in writing in two thousand years They'll

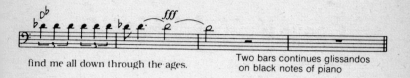

find me all down through the ages.

Two bars continues glissandos
on black notes of piano

I'M GLAD THAT I'M DEAD

SUE: I'm glad that I'm dead and never re-

turning I'm glad that I'm not in your shoes

There's nothing can touch me or bring me to

mourning For something as hopeless as you

BILL: Don't leave me behind without a prayer or a

rhyme I'm too young to go down like a dog

I've walked on hot coals I've branded the

mountains   I   can't just van- ish like the   fog

SUE: Good-bye darlin   Billy   This   land is too

lonesome   for someone who's   bigger than   life

I'm no   hero.   God knows.   and I   never   a-

spired   I was happy just being your   wife

(Stop)

COWBOY WALTZ

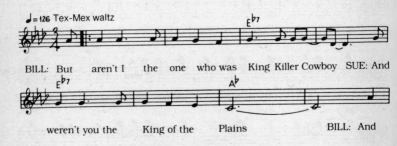

BILL: But   aren't I   the   one who was   King Killer Cowboy SUE: And

weren't you the   King of the   Plains   BILL: And

WHY IS WE BOTH DYIN

NOW I'M ALONE

but a   giant is only a kid   (Piano figure)

Cha-Cha boogie ♩=150 (change bass pattern)

So while you go shopping and watching TV   you can

ponder my vanishing shape   You can build   & tear them all down
                             your own mountains

But from death   you can't never escape

From death

you can't never   escape

END

THE SAD LAMENT OF PECOS BILL
ON THE EVE OF KILLING HIS WIFE

BILL: Oh why, on such a day as this
          My darlin Slue Foot Sue
          Did you force me wild and foolishly
          To be the cause of buryin you

SUE: It was my fate you saw me there
          Ridin high on the Rio Grande
          Atop some slimey catfish back
          You were callin for my hand

BILL: I was blinded by the sight of you
          No such a woman did exist
          I'd never seen the like of it
          Ridin high on some big old fish

SUE: But that was just the half of it
          For to marry was our demise
          If it hadn't been for takin oaths
          I'd be watchin that big sunrise

BILL: But wasn't it me
          Who taught the bronco how to buck

SUE: And wasn't it you
          Who roped tornados by the neck

BILL: And wasn't it me
          Who dug the mighty Rio Grande

SUE: All by hand

BOTH: All by hand
Then why is we both dyin
On this land
Why is we forsaken
Lost and shamed, forgotten
Why is we both rotten
In the memories of man
In the memories of man
In the memories of man

BILL: It was my mistake, I must admit
To introduce you to my horse
But I had heard such high acclaim
Of your horsemanship, of course

SUE: You coulda warned me first-handedly
Of the nature of your beast
I had no idea he was a killin bronc
Til he threw me sixty feet

BILL: You flew so high you cracked the sky
And was forced to duck the moon
I was mighty impressed but on the thirteenth
    time
I was singin a different tune

SUE: I was way high above, watchin you below
All the earth was a tiny speck
I was prayin for my second wind
I was prayin to save my neck

BILL: But wasn't it me
Who whipped the rattlesnake to death

SUE: Wasn't it you
Who invented the centipede

BILL: Wasn't it me
       Who dug the mighty Rio Grande

SUE: All by hand

BOTH: All by hand
       Then why is we both dyin
       On this land
       Why is we forsaken
       Lost and shamed, forgotten
       Why is we both rotten
       In the memories of man
       In the memories of man
       In the memories of man

BILL: It was three whole days
       And four whole nights
       And you were bouncin further still
       Out beyond the Milky Way
       But that bronc ain't had his fill

SUE: You called him "Widow Maker"
       But the reverse was comin true
       If I called him anything myself
       I'd a called the same to you

BILL: I was fadin fast inside my chest
       My poor head was all on fire
       I could not think but what to do
       So I pulled out that cold blue iron

SUE: You drew that gun way down below
       And I knew what you had in mind
       To fire upon your dear sweet wife
       Who was helplessly resigned

BOTH: Who was helplessly resigned to fate
       To die a hero's death
       It's the stuff that makes a legend great
       But the pain's still on our breath
       But the pain's still on our breath
       But the pain's still on our breath

BILL: I fired and fired like a devil-dog
       Shootin wildly in the sky
       And I saw my dear sweet Sue crash down
       Landin square on her naked eye

SUE: I was dead long before I hit the ground
       And I felt the stars like wind
       And I counted all my happy days
       On the back of a catfish fin

BILL: I could not let you buck like that
       Forever up and down
       For what's a married man to do
       Whose bride flies the day she's found

SUE: I ain't blamin you my darlin Bill
       It was in the hands of time
       To have me die a mortal's death
       And to die in a hero's prime

BILL: But it's me, ain't it me
       Who was so widely acclaimed

SUE: It's you, it was you
       Who was brave and true

BILL: It's me, ain't it me
       Who was so widely famed

SUE: And proclaimed throughout the land

BILL: It was me, it was me
        Who dug the mighty Rio Grande

SUE: And raised by the wild coyote

BILL: It was me, wasn't it me
        Who tamed the twisted hurricane

SUE: And he did it all by hand
        And he did it all by hand

BOTH: Then why is we both dyin
        On this land
        Why is we forsaken
        Lost and shamed, forgotten
        Why is we both rotten
        In the memories of man
        In the memories of man
        In the memories of man

BILL: Now you're dead and you're gone
        And I'm just passin on
        I can feel the cold sting of my guilt
        I look for a place to bury you, sweet
        But I'm buried as sure as you're kilt

SUE: Don't languish sweet Bill
        It's a poisonous pill
        What's done is all done and it's through
        Your crime was invented by lies of the mind
        It's a crime when a lie is so true

BILL: But I was fathered by liars
        And my offspring was too
        Oh how can I ever escape it
        To be born as a legend and die as a man
        It's painful to even relate it—

SUE: Be kind on yourself
        You won't last forever
        And the moon could care less what you do
        But don't forget *me* on the day that you saw me
        And how I was capturing you

BILL: But aren't I a hero
        Above all that stuff
        How could I just fall by the wayside
        I'm fixed in the prairies and valleys below me
        I'm fixed until heavens collide

SUE: You're vanishing Billy
        Just look at your breath
        Do you see it make ripples in space
        You're gone with the wind like others before
            you
        Not even leavin a trace
        Not even leavin a trace

BILL: But I'm bigger than mountains
        I'm bigger than time
        I'm written in history pages
        They'll find me in writing in two thousand
            years
        They'll find me all down through the ages.

SUE: I'm glad that I'm dead
        And never returning
        I'm glad that I'm not in your shoes
        There's nothing can touch me or bring me to
            mourning
        For something as hopeless as you

BILL: Don't leave me behind
        Without a prayer or a rhyme

I'm too young to go down like a dog
I've walked on hot coals and I've branded
    the mountains
I can't just vanish like the fog

SUE: Good-bye darlin Billy
This land is too lonesome
For someone who's bigger than life
I'm no hero, God knows, and I never aspired
I was happy just being your wife

BILL: But aren't I the one
Who was King Killer Cowboy

SUE: And weren't you the King of the Plains

BILL: And aren't I the one
Who strangled tornados

SUE: And twisted them into the rains

BILL: And aren't I the one
Who dug out the Badlands

SUE: And taught the wild bronc how to buck

BILL: And didn't I dig out
The whole damn Rio Grande

SUE: And you did it all by hand

BOTH: And we did it all by hand
Then why is we both dyin on this land

SUE: Why is we forsaken

BILL: Lost and shamed, forgotten

BOTH: Why is we both rotten
In the memories of man

In the memories of man
In the memories of man

BILL: And now I'm alone
On the desolate plains
Alone and drifting in space
My legend and time and my myth is forgot
So now you can look in my face

You can look in my eyeballs
Way back in my skull
You can wonder at all that I did
You can wonder at all of us miracle men
But a giant is only a kid

So while you go shopping
And watching TV
You can ponder my vanishing shape
You can build your own mountains and tear
Them all down
But from death you can't escape
From death you can't never escape

END